Write a Limerick - a humorous verse with a distinctive rhythm. The first, second, and fifth lines, the longer lines, rhyme. The third and fourth shorter lines rhyme. (A-A-B-B-A)

Cold Water – water so cold it is almost ice.
How much water is there? A glass? a bucket?
a lake?

What do you want but cannot have?

Write about something delicious you have eaten. Savour the taste, the smell, the sight, the touch of the food

Imagine being bathed in one color. What is that color and how does it make you feel?

Today is the day to challenge yourself to write an acrostic poem where the first, last or other letters in a line spell out a particular word or phrase

Something is out of place. Is a person, an object or a feeling?

How would a bird feel as it soars through the sky? What can it see from its lofty view?

Write a Sonnet

You physically bump into a stranger in a shop.
What happens next?

.

Write a poem about being selected for an elite sporting occasion.

You're gifted a trip in a helicopter. Are you excited? Anxious? What will you experience during the flight?

You can travel back in time and re-live one special day in your life..

Look in your fridge and pick an item from the very back that you had almost forgotton about. What memories or feelings might this item invoke?

A brilliant scientist has made an amazing breakthrough discovery. What might they feel at this moment?

You receive a piece of news that changes everything.

There's a knock at the door and an old friend is standing there. Someone who has not been seen for many years…

Write the final words of someone drawing their last breath

Write a shape poem where the words make a shape and also describe the shape being made.

Pick a celebrity and research their favorite things.

Write about someone new coming into your life. Are they good or bad for you?

The weather is unusual for the time of year – what is it like and how do people react?

Try writing a Japanese Senryu style poem. These have 3 lines and 17 syllables. Line 1 has 5 syllables, Line 2 has 7 syllables and Line 3 has 5 syllables.

It's so quiet. Everywhere is silent.

Write a poem about stroking the fur of an animal. What animal is it? Does the animal enjoy being stroked?

Something is happening and there is excitement in the air…

Think about a riddle. A riddle is a poem that describes something but leaves the reader to guess what it is that is being described.

Write about a toxic plant. Does it look toxic or benign? What happens if someone eats the plant?

You're an actor standing in the wings about to go on stage.

Pick a number and think what it is commonly associated with.

Think about an object you admire which is very old, older than you. Write about the life of this object.

Write a poem which is actually a recipe. This can be for a food item or maybe a spell or a tonic.

Think about a special item of clothing that signifies something to the wearer.

Write a short, satirical and witty poem – an epigram.

A friend is meeting up with you and they have some good news to impart.

You are the victim of a scam and you have just realized.

Write a poem about an 'Act Of God'.

Someone has betrayed you. Will you forgive them?

Let the word 'Lost' inspire you today.

You are the judge at a court case and the next chapter of people's lives depends on you.

A Kenning is a two word phrase describing an object often using a metaphor. Write a Kennings poem —a riddle composed of several lines of kennings to describe something or someone.

You find a box hidden in your home which you have never seen before.

Write about learning a new skill which is tricky to master.

Trapped in a lift. How did it happen? Who is with you if anyone and how will you escape?

It's a full moon and you are camping outside.
The whole area is bathed in moonlight.

You receive an interesting looking letter.

Write an Elegy. A lament for a loved one you have lost.

Advise a young child with a life lesson.

Write a gratitude poem giving thanks for something.

Are you perfect? Is anyone? How acceptable are flaws?

Write a poem that includes alliteration.

Take the first line of a poem you like and continue with the poem in your own style.

You are watching someone but they cannot see you. They are doing something they should not be doing.

You tip out the washing basket and there is something glinting amongst the pile of dirty clothes.

There is a ticket in your hand.

Describe an imaginary animal through the words of a poem.

Write about light and shadows. These can be real or metaphorical.

Imagine yourself at 5 years old. What is important to you?

Write a short poem about an image which enables the reader to see the image that you are describing.

Can you remember your feelings when you got your first car?

Describe a building that has been a big part of your life.

Imagine you are a King or Queen with many loyal subjects. Your wish is their command!

Write about a lie. Is the lie discovered? Why was the lie told? What are the consequences?

You have a key in the palm of your hand. Is it small or large? Weighty or light? What is it for?

You're hiding in a storm shelter. What are your hopes and fears?

There is a crackling noise. What is making the noise and how does it sound to you?

There is music coming from an upstairs open window. You can hear the music but not see the musician.

You enter a dark unfamiliar room and flick on the light switch.

The shop was full of brightly colored items.

Write a poem about a happy emotional feeling.

Write a poem to encourage someone to be brave.

You plunge your hand into dark, murky water and feel something jagged.

Compare night and day.

Create a poem inspired by an unusual musical instrument or something being used to create music that would not normally be used for this purpose.

Think about someone who uses a different name to their birth name and why this might be. They might have changed identity or just prefer a different name.

You are in a boring job and the hours stretch ahead of you. However, things are about to get exciting for a change!

There is a sign by the roadside. It's old and dilapidated but there is a reason for the sign.

You have a secret and know that you can't tell a soul.

Write about climbing a mountain. This can be real or metaphorical.

Write a rhyming poem that is actually a set of instructions.

Imagine a hoarder who struggles to move in their own home for all the items they have in there taking up all the space.

Someone asks for your help. You are the only person that can help them. How does that make you feel?

Write a poem about leaving something behind: school, an object, a person…

You are much smaller than normal. What problems does this pose and what opportunities?

You are the last guest left at a party. Describe the scene around you. What is your host doing?

Who is sitting in the waiting room? What are they doing to pass the time?

Create a poem about travelling on public transport. You could describe the sights and smells, the other passengers, the journey or the destination.

You are making your way through a dark forest but have a powerful flashlight to guide you. What do you discover?

Write about forgetting a computer password and the feelings this invokes.

Compose a poem to persuade someone to try a new food. Pick a food you love but that other people may be reticent about.

You have three coins in your pocket. What are they for?

Describe a tree bursting into life in Spring.

You blow the dust from an old book and you are surprised when you see the title of the book.

Someone has arrived at you home. They are here to help you with a specific task. Describe performing the task.

You are sitting in an old car. It has deep leather seats.

In your hand is a pair of sharp scissors. What is your intention?

Write a poem about the best season of the year.

There is a crowd of people. So many people that there is barely room to move and people are crushed up against each other.

You have won a prize. What did you have to do to win and what is the prize?

You find a book of poetry written by an ancestor of yours. What do you feel as you open the book.

Manufactured by Amazon.ca
Bolton, ON